LEARNING ABOUT THE EARTH
Prairies

by Hollie Endres

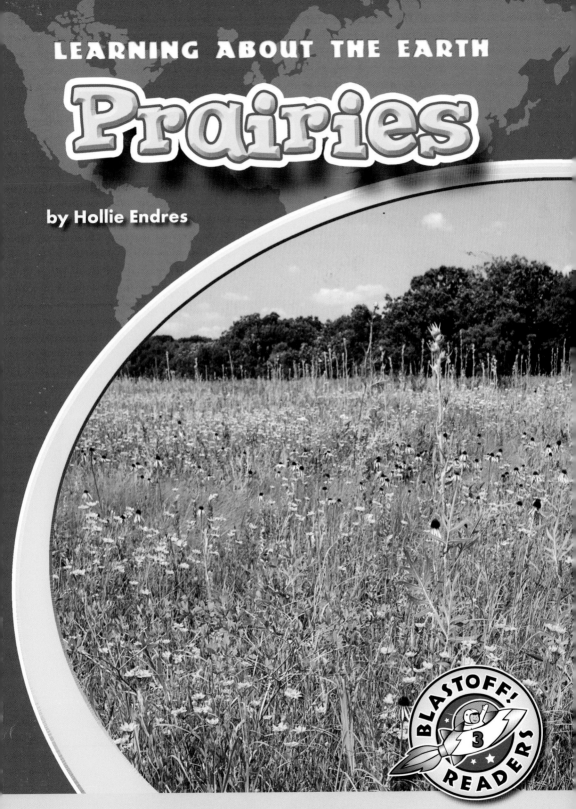

BLASTOFF!
3
READERS

BELLWETHER MEDIA • MINNEAPOLIS, MN

Note to Librarians, Teachers, and Parents:

Blastoff! Readers are carefully developed by literacy experts and combine standards-based content with developmentally-appropriate text.

Level 1 provides the most support through repetition of high-frequency words, light text, predictable sentence patterns, and strong visual support.

Level 2 offers early readers a bit more challenge through varied simple sentences, increased text load, and less repetition of high frequency words.

Level 3 advances early-fluent readers toward fluency through increased text and concept load, less reliance on visuals, longer sentences, and more literary language.

Level 4 builds reading stamina by providing more text per page, increased use of punctuation, greater variation in sentence patterns, and increasingly challenging vocabulary.

Level 5 encourages children to move from "learning to read" to "reading to learn" by providing even more text, varied writing styles, and less familiar topics.

Whichever book is right for your reader, Blastoff! Readers are the perfect books to build confidence and encourage a love of reading that will last a lifetime!

This edition first published in 2008 by Bellwether Media.

No part of this publication may be reproduced in whole or in part without written permission of the publisher. For information regarding permission, write to Bellwether Media Inc., Attention: Permissions Department, Post Office Box 1C, Minnetonka, MN 55345-9998.

Library of Congress Cataloging-in-Publication Data
Endres, Hollie J.
  Prairies / by Hollie Endres.
    p. cm. – (Blastoff! readers. Learning about the earth)
Summary: "Simple text and supportive images introduce beginning readers to the physical characteristics and geographic locations of Prairies"—Provided by publisher.
  Includes bibliographical references and index.
  ISBN-13: 978-1-60014-114-0 (hardcover : alk. paper)
  ISBN-10: 1-60014-114-5 (hardcover : alk. paper)
  1. Prairies–Juvenile literature. 2. Prairie ecology–Juvenile literature. I. Title.

QH87.7.E53 2008
578.74'4–dc22   2007014943

Contents

Prairies are large areas of grassland. Few trees grow in prairies.

Most prairies are flat.
Some prairies have
low hills.

Grasses are the most important plants on prairies. There are hundreds of different kinds of grasses.

Grasses need water to grow. They grow to be only a few inches high in places that do not get much rain.

Grasses are taller where more rain falls. They can grow much taller than you!

Prairie grasses have deep roots. The roots pull water from underground.

Grasses mix with soil to form
a tangled layer called **sod**.

Sod covers the ground like a blanket. It keeps roots from freezing in winter. Roots that stay alive all winter can send up new plants in the spring.

Wildflowers also grow in prairies. Many wildflowers bloom in spring. Colorful flower blossoms mix with the green grasses.

Prairie plants grow taller during summer.

Prairie plants dry up and turn golden shades of red and yellow in the fall.

The dry plants are often fuel for **wildfires**. Prairies need fire. It burns away dead plants and makes way for new plants to grow.

The prairie is home to many animals. **Bison graze** on grasses.

Coyotes hunt other prairie animals such as rabbits and mice.

Prairie dogs make their homes underground in some prairies. They dig tunnels and rooms to make prairie dog towns.

Prairies once covered the middle of North America. People dug up the rich prairie soil to plant **crops**. Other prairie land became **pastures** for animals.

Today there are few prairies left. Some have been saved as nature **preserves**.

Some people
plant grasses and
wildflowers to
make prairies. They
want to return the
land to the way it
was long ago.

Glossary

bison—a large and shaggy animal that lives on North American prairies

coyote—a North American animal related to wolves

crops—plants grown by people for food

graze—to eat grass growing on land

pasture—grazing land for animals

prairie dog—a small animal related to a squirrel

preserve—an area set aside to be protected in its original state; preserves help protect land and animals.

sod—soil held together by matted plants and roots

wildfire—a large fire that spreads fast and is hard to put out; wildfires are often started when lightning hits the ground.

wildflower—a flower that grows without the help of people

To Learn More

AT THE LIBRARY
Bannatyne-Cugnet, Jo. *A Prairie Alphabet.*
Plattsburgh, N.Y.: Tundra Books, 1992.

Bouchard, David. *If You're Not from the Prairie.* New
York: Atheneum Books for Young Readers, 1995.

Collard, Sneed. *Butterfly Count.* New York: Holiday
House, 2002.

Johnson, Rebecca L. *A Walk in the Prairie.*
Minneapolis, Minn.: Carolrhoda Books, 2001.

Salzmann, Mary Elizabeth. *On the Prairie.* Edina,
Minn.: Abdo, 2001.

Wallace, Marianne D. *America's Prairies and
Grasslands.* Golden, Colo.: Fulcrum Resources,
2001.

ON THE WEB
Learning more about prairies
is as easy as 1, 2, 3.

1. Go to www.factsurfer.com

2. Enter "prairies" into search box.

3. Click the "Surf" button and you will see a list of
   related web sites.

With factsurfer.com, finding more information is just a
click away.

Index

The photographs in this book are reproduced through the courtesy of: Steve Geer, front cover; Eva Serrabassa, pp. 4-5; Bogdfan Radenkovic, pp. 6-7; Duncan Walker, pp. 8-9; Derek Croucher/Alamy, p. 10; Vicki France, p. 11; Super Stock/agefotostock, pp. 12-13; Gareth McCormack/Alamy, p. 14; Mark O. Thiessen/Getty Images, p. 15; Enrique R. Aguirre/agefotostock, p. 16; Sebastian Burel, p. 17; Roger Dale Calger, p. 18; Cheryl Casey, p. 19; Danita Delimont/Alamy, pp. 20-21.